Sitting At His Feet

By Joanne Ellison

ISBN-13: 978-0-9971243-1-6

DEDICATION

This book is dedicated to my son Billy who encouraged me to write a devotional to help people during stressful times.

TABLE OF CONTENTS

PREFACE

Do you hunger for more of Jesus?
Come, sit at His feet, and hear His voice
as He leads you to still waters and
restores your soul.

INTRODUCTION

I am often asked how to read Scripture. My response is to allow the Word to read you, to have the Word speak to you as a love letter from God the Father. When I read Scripture, I ask the Lord to speak to me through His Word and journal what I sense He is saying to me.

This book is a compilation of journal entries from my personal quiet times with the Lord. These writings come out of my wrestling through issues with Him in the Word and in prayer and the comfort He has given me in the process. They come from a heart to heart meeting with the Lord.

The entries are grouped by subject so that you can quickly access a writing that addresses an area of struggle or growth. I have purposely kept this book short to provide a small guide that can be kept at your fingertips for moments of need. Each writing is followed by a list of Scripture verses for further reading. As you read the Scripture, ask the Lord to speak to you through His Word.

My hope is that the journal entries and accompanying Scripture would encourage you in your journey with the Lord and act as a catalyst to take you deeper into the Word and into His presence and deeper in your response to Him. As you seek Him with all of your heart, soul, strength, and mind, may you find His Word to be the water that cleanses the heart; may it illumine the dark places of life, bring forth truth and conviction, give hope, and restore the soul; may it be a lamp to your feet and a light to your path.

In the process, may you draw near to the Lord and enjoy the fruit of living from a place of resting in His presence. As you may remember in the familiar story from chapter 10 of Luke, we see the contrast between two sisters—one who is busy working for Jesus and one who is resting in Jesus. Jesus is the honored guest at the home of his friends Martha and Mary. Martha is busy making preparations in the kitchen, but Mary squeezes in close to Jesus and sits at His feet. Martha was up to her elbows bearing the load of preparation, but Mary chose something better. She chose to partake in the real feast. The banqueting table that was set before her was the Presence of Christ. She heard a new sound; her spiritual ears and eyes were opened. She feasted on His Words and knew that the water He offered would quench her spiritual thirst. Do you hunger for more of Jesus? Come, sit at His feet, and hear His voice as He leads you to still waters and restores your soul. God bless you as you journey with me into the hope that God brings and as you discover His great love for you.

ANGER

Why do you spend your precious time being angry? Yes, you have been wronged, and I see the wrong done to you. But I have instructed you in my Word not to sin in your anger. Your anger may be justified, but sin will squeeze into a place in your life when you hold onto your anger. Let me exchange your anger for my peace. Let me carry the burden of the hurt and pain because in my hands your anger can become a place of love and growth. If you continue to hold onto it, you will find yourself bitter. And the space where I wish to dwell will be crowded out. Come to me in your weariness and pain, and I will exchange your anger for rest. Trust me. I am confident that you will see the fruit of letting go.

Ephesians 4:26-27; James 1:19-20; Romans 12:17-21

Anger

Resist the temptation to get even with those who have wronged you. Retaliation is the enemy's playground. He prowls around looking for a place in your life to trap you into sin. Anger is a God given emotion that when used properly can motivate you to make corrections in your life. But anger unchecked can lead to sin. Settle offenses quickly. Deal with the wrong; forgive the offender and do not take the bait of retaliation. The more that you know my perfect love and receive my understanding in a matter, the easier it will become to deal with the offense my way—the way of love. I will lead you beside the still waters and restore your hurt soul. Forgiveness is the highway to freedom.

Matthew 6:12-14; I Peter 5:8; Ephesians 4:26

ANXIETY

For years anxiety has found a place in your heart. I know that even as a child you found anxiety to be a faithful companion. But anxiety is the counterfeit of peace. Where anxiety and fear dwell, my peace becomes only a sidelined player in the game of your life. I am known as the Prince of Peace because I am perfect peace. When you surrender your anxious thoughts to me, I will replace those thoughts with my Word. My Word is truth and brings my peace. You can be certain that my Word, when dwelling richly in your heart, will keep anxiety in the outfield of your life. I sent you the Holy Spirit to comfort, direct, and counsel you so that anxiety will have no place in your life. My Spirit directs you in the way you should go, and my love comforts you in your hour of need. There are many paths you can take in life but the path of life—true life—can only be found in me. My path is laden with the promises of my Word along the way. Meditate on my Word to redirect your thoughts and find the path of peace.

Isaiah 12:2; Isaiah 26:3-4; John 14:27-28; Philippians 4:6-8; 2 Peter 1:4

Anxiety

I see that anxiety has found its way into the space where I desire to dwell. Your anxiety has filled your internal space with thoughts that are not my thoughts and ways that are not my ways. I have not deposited within you anxiety; that is the counterfeit of my peace. Take a look at the root of your anxiety. My Word to you is to be anxious for nothing. I care about every hair on your head. I watch your every move and lead you to the place of freedom from the cares of this world. The world can cause anxiety but my children bear the mark of peace and contentment, not as the world gives, but a peace that only I can give. Come close to me; sit with me; talk to me and I will listen. Lay down your anxious thoughts and agree with me that I am your Paraclete, the One who comes alongside you and cares for you. This is a better way, a road less traveled but a road filled with hope.

I Peter 5:7; Luke 10:41; Luke 12: 25-26; John 14:27

Anxiety

Do not be anxious. Turn your anxiety into praise and thanksgiving. Draw near to me with a grateful heart. David, my anointed king, understood the power of praise and thanksgiving and reminded my people to enter the courts with thanksgiving and praise. He knew the key to my presence is praise. I am not an egocentric God but a God who draws near when you praise me. When you run after other gods like power, people, money, or prestige you are giving praise and value to these things. Come and seek me and you will find rest and peace. Praise and worship will turn anxiety into joy. My peace will flow from you like a river when you turn your attention to me alone. Circumstances may not change, but your ability to rise above the circumstances will set anxiety to flight and create a new song in your heart.

Psalm 103:1-3; I Peter 5:7-8; Philippians 4:6-7

BROKEN RELATIONSHIPS

People will often let you down. Disappointments come in the most unexpected ways and from unexpected people. If you put your hope in people, they will disappoint you. Your hope must be wholly in me. I will never disappoint you. I am your advocate. My ways are not your ways and my thoughts are not your thoughts. My ways are higher. I see the bigger picture of your hurt and pain. I see the higher yes. As you turn to me I will show you a better way to live above circumstances and pain. The place of your brokenness today will be your strength tomorrow. Keep your eyes on me and give me your pain. I will carry it for you and take you to a place of freedom.

Isaiah 55:8-9; 2 Corinthians 4:16-18; Hebrews 12:2

Broken Relationships

You have hoped that your love would not fail—that if you did the right thing, if you opened your heart and forgave, all would be made right. But this significant relationship is ebbing away. You are unable to control the actions of the one whom you love. You hoped things would change and the relationship would be repaired. Beloved, this is out of your control. Man's free will, which offers love freely to me, is the same free will that withdraws his love. Let go of what you hoped would be and look to what will be as I take the pain of this broken relationship and lead you beside still waters. You cannot control others, but you can control your willingness to come to me. My words to the woman at the well are true for you today. Come to me, the Living Water, that you might be refreshed, filled, and find hope.

Psalm 55:22; Isaiah 55:1; John 4:7-14

BUSYNESS

Are you aware that busyness takes you from me? It steals your time and your energy and threatens to overtake you. B-U-S-Y—*Being –Under-Satan's-Yoke.* My child, when you stay on the hamster wheel of busyness, you end up under Satan's yoke. Release yourself from the pressure of perfectionism and drivenness. My desire for you is to be fruitful not busy. When you are fruitful you have been abiding in me, the Vine. I know the plans I have for you for good, and my plans do not include stress. My plans are for your perfect peace as you seek my will. Keep in step with me and follow my lead. I will lead you in the way that you should go and not push or drive you. I will gently lead you beside still waters. When you take the path that I have chosen for you, you will find freedom and peace. Stress induced followers are not surrendered followers. Surrender your plans, and I will show you a new way to live in me.

Isaiah 26:3; Luke 10:38-42; John 15:7-8

DEPRESSION

My child, I know you think that I have deserted you. The overwhelming feeling of loss and heartache threatens to overtake you. I once had a friend named David who had to run from a mad King Saul. There were days when he cried out to me. I answered, but he could not hear my still small voice. Fear and anxiety crowded out my voice, but I did not abandon him. His agony turned into depression until one day my voice broke through. One day David remembered. He remembered that I had promised never to forsake him even in his darkest hour and that I was with him wherever he went. And in remembering he recalled my name: I AM. I am not the God of *I was* or the God of *I will be.* I AM. And when he remembered I was there, when he became still and heard my voice, the oppression lifted. Turn to me my friend. I am the only One who sticks closer to you as a brother.

Exodus 3:13-15; Proverbs 18:24; Psalm 142:5-12

DESPAIR

You seem to have lost your bearings like a ship tossed out at sea. The anchor lifted, and despair found its way into your soul. Despair strikes like a sudden storm that catches you unaware. One minute you are fine and the next minute you find yourself tossed in the raging sea of emotions. Life in the Garden was designed to be stress free. Humanity has been fighting his way back to the Garden ever since. For now my child, you live in the time of my kingdom having come and my kingdom yet to be fulfilled. In this in-between time do not despair. I have overcome the world. I have given you my Holy Spirit to lead you into truth, to come alongside you. Do not despair as this trial threatens to overtake you. Follow my lead into the eye of the storm. Though the storm may not calm for the moment, I will lead you to the place of peace amidst the storm.

Psalm 27:12-14; John 16:33; 2 Corinthians 4:7-8; Hebrews 6:19-20

Despair

In the quietness of your heart I dwell. As you make space for my voice you will begin to see the plans that I have for you that are good. What the enemy intends for evil I will turn for good. Your misplaced hope is causing you to despair, and I long for you to hear my voice of hope. I see you tuning in to so many other voices that promote despair and take away your hope. The only certainty you can have in this life is the certainty that I am faithful. I was with my apostle Paul when he was beaten, shipwrecked, and locked in prison. His life in me threatened every power of darkness that is opposed to the fulfillment of my plans. But even Paul was able to say that neither life nor death, things present, nor things to come could separate him from my love. And nothing is able to stand against my love for you either. Paul's relationship with me enabled him to continue to press on despite the force of despair that continuously assaulted him. My relationship with you can do the same. It will sustain you in your darkest hour of need. I am here to replace despair with eternal hope.

Romans 8:28; Psalm 27:13-14; I Peter 5:6-7

DESTINY

I have a plan and purpose for your life. Do not despair that your life has no purpose. You have great purpose. I knew you before you were born. In me alone are you complete. As you seek me and grow in the knowledge of me, your unique destiny will be revealed. Each step that you take closer to me will help you to discover who you are in the light of My Presence. Do not waste time in wondering or asking what you are to do. I will lead you in the way that you are to go. Your mission must be to seek me and your heart's desires will be revealed.

Psalm 32:7-8; Jeremiah 1:5; Ephesians 2:10

Destiny

My purposes alone will stand. There are many plans that my people make, and yet it is only *my plans* that will stand the test of time. Seek my kingdom and my righteousness, and my plans will unfold for you. I have my eyes on you. I see how you delight in me and seek me in your daily life. Take my hand and follow me as I lead you beside still waters and open doors through which you may walk. There will be a day when you will look back at your life and see that my hand has been upon you leading and guiding. Do not second guess my plans for you. Simply seek me.

Isaiah 42:16; Jeremiah 29:13-14; Psalm 23:2

Destiny

If you delight in me I will give you the desires of your heart. As you find your joy in me alone you will find that your desires will change. You will begin to want what I want, see what I see, hear what I hear. Your desires will be transformed by my desires and they will be fulfilled. My child, it is my purposes for your life that are the best for you. It may seem that your gifts are not being used for my glory. You may feel like you have no purpose. Do not underestimate the purpose of seeking me. In the process, you will begin to walk in your destiny. I will show you greater things than you could imagine and will take you to heights you never anticipated.

Psalm 37:3-5; Romans 12:1-2; Ephesians 3:20

Destiny

Why do you despair my child? Trust me as I lead you to higher ground. Your heart is set on doing great things for my kingdom ,and I know that you will. But remember it is I who must lead you on this chosen path. I have things that I need to deposit into your life —character for you to sustain the call. There is work yet to be done to empower you to embrace your destiny. Do not be in a hurry to accomplish my work. Live daily in the light of my Presence, and you will find fulfillment. You are not waiting to accomplish great things. You are accomplishing great things as you wait.

John 15:4; Ephesians 4:13; 2 Peter 1:5-7

Destiny

Open your eyes my child and see the beauty of the world that I created. My name, Elohim, Creator God painted the stars in the sky and the moon and the sun. I created the first man, Adam, and then his companion, Eve. I created them to love me and to receive my love and from that intense place of security they could love each other. I created you in your mother's womb. You are not an accident but my precious child. You have purpose and were chosen to step out in faith using the gifts that I have given you. Your strength is in your dependency on me,for where you think you are weak is where I can strengthen you. My purposes stand, and my desire is that you look to me for your future. Do not make plans without me. I have the higher plan for your life. Seek me every day and I will lead you into your destiny.

Genesis 1:1; Psalm 139:13; John 15:16

Destiny

Do not be dismayed at the fiery trial you are undergoing. I am with you and will never leave you. I have seen your disappointment and heard your plea for help. But I want you to understand that nothing gets by my loving hands. I will take your disappointments and turn them into *divine appointments*. I will lead you to the plans and purposes I have for you. Each trial is an opportunity to strengthen you and bring you closer to your destiny. I am a loving Father who will lead you into places you never imagined. Your thinking is too small. I see your future and if you will trust me you will go to places you could hardly imagine and do great things in my name. I am not looking for opportunities for you. I am taking you to doors that are already open as you seek my Name. Do not place your trust in man's plans. Seek my highest plan for your life.

I Peter 4:12-13; I Peter 5:10; James 1:12

FAITH

My call on your life is unfolding as you exercise your faith. Your faith is not blind faith; your faith is based on knowledge of me. Faith comes from hearing my Word. If you will tune into my voice, you will hear me speaking. I long for you to hear the secrets I have reserved for those who spend time in my secret chamber—the place of intimacy where your faith in me will grow. My Word to you will be like a lamp to your feet and a light to your path. There was a day when I met a man named Zacchaeus. He was a tax collector straining to catch a glimpse of me and hear my words. I called Zacchaeus out of the tree, and, in amazement, he came down and followed me. He did not know it at the time, but his faith, though stretched, became the opportunity for him to know me intimately. There were others who were once observers. You might call them fans today. But when they stepped out in faith, they went from being a fan at a distance to becoming a follower. Climb out of the tree my friend. The distance between us is too vast. Come down. I want to share my secrets with you.

Psalm 119:105; Proverbs 3:5; Romans 10:17; Luke 19:1-10

Faith

Open your eyes and look at the earth that I created. The beauty of the earth is evidence that I exist. I am Elohim, The Creator, and nothing has escaped my eye. You are evidence of my best creation. I saved the best for last. Look in the mirror and marvel at my most magnificent creation. When your faith in yourself fails, remember that it is I who created you in your mother's womb. I determined your destiny and know every hair on your head. I see that your faith has failed. You are unsure of yourself, but I am the one who allowed your failure in order to turn you towards me. You are my child and I have your best interest in mind always. I am calling you out of self-sufficiency and into dependence on me. I am not like those who undermine your trust. I am always faithful, always dependable, and always available. My heart's desire is for you to lean on me by faith so that I can enable and empower you to fulfill your destiny. As you learn to depend on me, you will see problems solved that seemed unsolvable, hearts softened that seemed forever hardened, causes empowered that seemed hopeless.

Proverbs 3:5; Psalm 139: 1-14; Romans 10:17; I Corinthians 1:9

Faith

Keep your eyes on me. The challenge is to look up and not down at your circumstances. I stand at the door knocking for you to let me into the secret place of your thought life. My Word to you will bring perspective on what troubles you. My Word will bring clarity to your thoughts. The circumstance that is so stressful has an outcome that can either involve me or not. Bring me into the place of the heavy load and let me do the heavy lifting. Your faith is not dependent on what *you* can do. Your faith is dependent on what *I* can do. Exercising your faith muscles involves your letting go and trusting that I have your back. Your striving and stressing to solve the problem is wearing you out. I never called you to overcome life; I called you to life overcoming. Life overcoming is possible because I did the heavy lifting on the cross. Give me your burden, and, in so doing, your faith will increase.

Matthew 11:28-30; Psalm 46

Faith

You must learn to see with the eyes of your heart. When you look at what is and calculate your understanding based on this, you will lose my higher understanding—that which I give by faith. When you seek me as you go throughout your day, you will find me everywhere. I am with you at your job. I am with you in your home and in your relationships. Seek me by calling on the Holy Spirit to open the eyes of your heart so that you can walk by faith and not by sight. I long to show you what is behind the harsh words others speak or the anger behind your co-workers words. I long to show you the hurt in others so that you can be my hands and feet. When you learn to walk by faith, you will see and hear the sounds of heaven and be able to bring heaven to earth.

I Chronicles 16:11; Ephesians 4:2-3; 2 Corinthians 5:6-7

Faith

As you walk by faith, your faith will increase. My Word defines faith as the assurance of things hoped for, the evidence of the unseen. The men and women of God who believed in me exercised faith, and many never saw the fruit of their obedience. Yet these men and women persevered fighting the good fight. I am aware of the journey you are on as you seek to find me, as you wait in expectation to see in the physical what you see with your eyes of faith. I am calling you out of a place of waiting and into the place of fulfillment. The object of your faith is found in me and through me and with me. Take my hand and enjoy our journey together. My friend Peter, impetuous as he was, nevertheless became a great man of faith. It was difficult for him to wait. Impatience sometimes caused him to walk by sight when I had called him to trust me. Follow me with your eyes of faith.

II Corinthians 5:7; Hebrews 11

FEAR

Fear has some stubborn traveling companions. Fear travels in circles that compete for your peace and drive stress. His buddies are stress, insecurity, and anxiety. His circle of friends threatens to overtake you as you examine the possibilities set before you. Do not fear the future or even the snares of today. Look to me for the solutions to your problems. Fear is a clawless lion that growls loud enough to cause you to get stressed and anxious. Fear confronted with my love stands no chance of survival; my perfect love drives out fear. When you open your heart to my love, surrendering to the endless possibilities that my love will bring, fear must go. Fear has taken residence in your heart in the space where my love longs to dwell. As you seek my love and stand against the fear, you will find that fear has no sting. No matter what you face each day—a health issue, even a sentence of death, fear cannot stand against my love.

Psalm 23:4; I John 4:17-18; I Peter 5:7-8

Fear

It is tempting to give in to fear my child, but fear is the counterfeit to my peace. I know the fear that consumes you, but look to me to replace your fear with my peace and hope. Many years ago I reminded my people, the Israelites, that when they passed through the waters they would not be overtaken, and when they walked through the fire I would be with them. I was with Daniel in the lion's den and with him and his companions in the fiery furnace. When your problems cause you to be afraid remember that I am with you; that no matter what you face I will be with you. The basis of fear is the sense of being alone, so knowing that I am with you displaces the root of fear. My hands are not tied behind my back and neither are yours. You have choices you can make because I go before you. Release your fear to me and seek my face. I will lead you to my perfect peace.

Isaiah 43:1-2; Daniel 6:19-20; 2 Corinthians 1:9-10

FORGIVENESS

My child, you must learn not to take the bait of offense. The enemy is looking for ways to cause you to fall. He does not want you to prosper. Each time you take the bait of offense he leads you into a vulnerable place of anger and bitterness. When offenses come your way remember Joseph who was thrown into the pit by his brothers. They were jealous of him and they chose to be rid of him. When the opportunity to get even with them presented itself, Joseph rose above the offenses and hurts and forgave them. He was able to do this because he continually looked at what I was doing and not what others were doing to him. He chose the *highway* of forgiveness and not the way of bitterness. When you keep your eyes on me and offenses come your way, you will be able to take the way of love.

Mathew 6:14-15; Ephesians 4:31-32; Colossians 3:13

HOPE

When you wait upon me you will find hope. You will soar like an eagle. Place your plans and your hope in me, and you will find the assurance you are looking for—not self assurance but God assurance. You will find that waiting on me to move in your life has awesome benefits. Your faith will increase as you wait on me and your hope, rightfully placed on me, will produce fruit in your life. Hope deferred can make your heart sick. If you will trust me and wait on my perfect timing, you will find your desires realized. I see your frustration as you wait on my promises and for things to change in your life. But I am growing trust and faith in you so that when your hope is realized you will be able to sustain the growth. I am growing deep roots of hope in your heart and the challenge you face in waiting will produce a much larger harvest in your life than shallow roots.

Isaiah 40:31; Jeremiah 17:7-8; Proverbs 13:12

HOPELESSNESS

My precious child, you are not meant to live under your circumstances but above your circumstances. I have called you out of the pit and into my loving arms. I have spoken my Word to you that I uphold you, that my arms are open wide to you. The enemy is feeding you his lies that there is no hope. But look up my child. I am here to bring you a word of hope and encouragement. I have set your feet on secure paths that I have chosen. I have a purpose for your life that no one can snatch because it is I who created you in your mother's womb. I have deposited in you my hope. Reach out to me. I will not desert you in your time of despair. I am the Promise Keeper. Even if your life seems shipwrecked, I am Master over the storms of life. I say to the waters, "*Be still,*" and they must obey. As you look to me, you will find a hope that is not based on circumstances changing or on people who will disappoint you. Your hope will be found in me alone, the Rock of all ages.

Proverbs 23:18; Proverbs 25:3-5; Psalm 37:9; Psalm 139:13

Hopelessness

I know the days I have planned for you. I know the endless possibilities of things that we can do together, but hopelessness is stealing your joy. I have heard you say, " Life is not worth living." My child you are mine. Nothing can separate you from my love and the hope that I bring to your life. My plans are greater than anything you can imagine, and with me there is fullness of joy. Your circumstances that are making you lose hope are not the defining moments of your life. What defines your life is *Christ in you, the hope of glory*. If you put your hope in people or in the outcome you desire, you will be disappointed. People will let you down. Life is filled with circumstances that steal your joy, but my hope springs eternal. The hope that I bring is a wellspring, a fountain that never runs dry. The key to restoration of hope is to drink from the fountain of my Word. Drink frequently and plentifully. I will restore your hope.

Isaiah 40:28-31; Jeremiah 29:11; Psalm 3:2-6

INSECURITY

The enemy of your soul wants you to be insecure. He whispers his lies causing you to lose hope and become insecure. Remember my child that you can only be secure in my arms listening to my words. My Word is a book of hope to you, a lamp to your path, and light to your feet. I shine just enough light on to your path for you to be dependent on me. If you get to far ahead of me, you will lose your way. Day by day, step-by-step, I lead you away from the troublesome waters of insecurity and on to the path of surety, the path that I have chosen for you. I have great plans for you fashioned not by the hands of man but by the hand of God. I know every hair on your head and created you to be secure in the path that I have chosen for you. Follow me.

Isaiah 54:17; Psalm 119:105; Philippians 1:6

Insecurity

The only secure place in life is your life hidden in me. Your identity can only be found in me. Your job, your friends, family, prestige or possessions do not define you. All of these things, though gifts from me, nevertheless do not define your life. If you lean on people or things to give you happiness or security you will not be at peace. You will find yourself running after the wind and chasing a false sense of fulfillment. It is my unconditional love that defines your life. As you yield to my love you will find a joy that is deep within you. You will find the answers that you long for to the questions that invade your thoughts. Every question find's its answer in me. Turn to me and receive my love. Remember you are fearfully and wonderfully made in my image.

Psalm 23:1; Proverbs 139:14; Philippians 4:19

Insecurity

I once told my disciples a story about sinking sand. They listened in amazement but they did not fully comprehend the depth of the story until I had left them. I told them that they must build their house on the rock. I am the Rock; all else is sinking sand. If you build your house on your reputation, relationships, or possessions, it will fall. Security is built on me. I am the Rock of Salvation, the sure foundation that you can build on. I am the Cornerstone, the beginning and end of all truth. When you build your life on me, in me, and through me, you will find security. Anything else is false security. My dear friend Peter was impetuous. He loved me, but he was not grounded in me. When I left this earth, He denied me and ran. But when I appeared again I found Him and restored him. From that time on he built his life on me, the Rock. I became his firm foundation. Then he was able to proclaim my gospel fearlessly because he was secure in my love.

Psalm 127:1; Matthew 7:24-27; Ephesians 2:20

LONELINESS

I am the Alpha and Omega, the beginning and the end. I was; I am and I will be forever. Eternity is my home and I long to take up residence in your spiritual temple. I long for you to make space for me to drive out your loneliness and become aware of my Presence. I long to inhabit the places that have taken up space in your life where I belong. As long as you define yourself as abandoned and unloved, loneliness will be your name. But I have called you out of the wilderness and into the garden of my Presence. I have called you out of the place of thirst and into the place of Living Water. I have changed your name from Desolate to Desire. You are my desire, my bride with whom I long to dwell. Will you make me your habitation, your dwelling place? It may be difficult for you to allow me to change your name because you have become accustomed to being lonely. But that is not who you are. Surrender your counterfeit name and become my bride. I will fill the longing in your heart to be loved.

Isaiah 41:10; Isaiah 62:3-4; Matthew 11:28; I Corinthians 6:19-20; Revelation 1:8

Loneliness

There is a river that runs throughout my Word, the Holy Scripture. From Genesis to Revelation, that river brings life. From the beginning to the end, you will find my river never ceasing. I am the Word. I am the Living Water. I once met a woman by a well in Samaria. My heart broke for her as I watched her drawing water all by herself in the heat of the day. She was alone and rejected. She was shocked when I spoke to her asking her to please draw water from the well. As we conversed I told her that I had water I could give her, water that would cause her never to thirst again. I told her that I was the Living Water. She was uncertain at first and questioned me about worshiping on another mountain. How difficult it was for her to comprehend what I was trying to tell her. I am Living

Water. When you drink of me you will not thirst; you will not need to feel alone or rejected. Your friends may reject you. Your enemies will surely reject you. But I offer you the refreshing water of my life—water that will fill your emptiness and heal the wound of rejection. Come to me and drink.

Isaiah 43:1-5; Isaiah 55:1-2; John 4:7-14; John 7:38

Loneliness

This trial that clouds your vision will one day be a distant memory. The stress of walking through this has caused you to pull away from those who love you the most. It is easy to fall into the lie that no one cares and that you must walk this out by yourself. The enemy of your soul prowls around seeking to devour you and drive you further away from those who are willing to help. I have not designed my people to live alone. I created Eve for Adam, I and designed a community of believers to be available to you. This crisis does not define you and it does not need to overtake you with the fear of being alone. Look around at those I have placed in your life to help you. My friend

Moses needed his friends to hold up his hands when he went through the battle. I used his uplifted hands to bring victory but only with the help of his friends was he able to endure and triumph.

Exodus 17:11-12; Ecclesiastes 4:9-10; I Peter 5:8

PEACE

I will give you a peace that transcends understanding. In the midst of your trials and anxiety, I will give you hope. Turn back to me and seek me with all of your heart. Your circumstances seem to be spinning out of control, but I am the eye of the storm. And I am the Prince of Peace. There is river of life with my Presence that constantly flows and is available to you. No trial or difficulty can keep you from my Presence. My peace is available to you like a river that is teeming with life—my life. It is my love that never fails that will keep you centered on me and not on the trial. If only you would turn back to me and surrender to the river of my Presence, you will find that you no longer have to tread water but can float in the river of my life.

Isaiah 26:3; Isaiah 48:17-18; Psalm 46:10

REPENTANCE

Turn from the sin that blocks our relationship and turn back to me. I long for you to return to me. My love is constant and I miss the times you used to spend with me. I am not an angry, harsh Father. I am the loving Father who sent my Son, Jesus Christ to bring you back to me. He made a way on the cross for you to come back to me. Your sin has separated you from me. I have not left you; you have left me. When you turn back to me, you will be refreshed and cleansed. I long to tell you the secrets of my heart, but your heart is occupied with this sin. I am the great Surgeon who will heal your heart and restore you to good health. I stand at the door knocking.

Isaiah 59:1-2; Matthew 3:2-3; Acts 3:19; Revelation 3:20

Repentance

What do you fear my child? Are you afraid that I will not take you back because you have strayed from me? There was once a young man who left his father's house and squandered his inheritance. His Father's arms were opened wide when he returned home destitute and defeated. I am your loving Father awaiting your return. My arms are open and always ready for you to turn back to me. The struggle of sin will not overtake you. My power is more than enough to help you to overcome the strain of the pressures that you face. My Son Jesus Christ looked down from the cross and said, "*Father forgive them.....*" He bought your forgiveness at a high price—His life—because of His great love for you. His arms are open.

Luke 4:18; Luke 15:18-24; Romans 7:14

Repentance

Your ways are not my ways; your thoughts are not my thoughts. Turn back to me so that you will be able to hear me whisper to you in the secret place. Surrender to me and your heart will soften to know my thoughts and my ways. You have wondered if I am a distant God. The distance between us exists because of your straying from me not from my leaving. King David, after his sin with Bathsheba, recognized that his sin was against me. But when he turned back to me his heart became softened again; he could hear my voice again. My life is hidden in you and my thoughts are available to you to bring you comfort and help. Do you believe that the plans I have for you are always for good? I long for you to understand my ways, yet my ways are blocked when your heart is hardened. Sin threatens to keep you from me, but "*lo I am with you always even unto the ends of the earth.*" Turn back to me.

Psalm 51:1-4; Proverbs 28: 13-14; Matthew 28:20

Repentance

It is finished. What is it about my final words on the cross that defy your understanding? The work of the cross is complete; nothing left to do. When you come to me for forgiveness it is done and your sin is washed away. As I hung on the cross I was not defeated. I willingly lay down my life so that you could have life. I know you feel shame and guilt. I took on your shame and guilt on the cross.

Turn away from the past and turn towards me. I have forgiven you and now you need to forgive yourself and accept my words "*It is finished.*" My intention is to take you to a new place—to lead you as The Great Shepherd to green pastures and pure water. I have plans for your life as you return to me. There is nothing or no one who can cause you to stay on the sidelines of life. In me you have new life. Today is the beginning of your new life in me.

Colossians 2:13-14; 2 Corinthians 5: 18-19; 2 Corinthians 7:9-1

REST

I know that you are worn out and have resisted giving in to much needed rest. I long to bear your burden and take from you the heavy yoke of stress. My yoke is easy and burden light. When you release the concerns that you carry to me you will find rest. I have the answers that you need and the plan to navigate this trial. When you come to me I will take the heavy backpack of worry and the concerns that you have and carry them for you. Have you forgotten that I give strength to the weary and am your greatest advocate? I will lead you in the way that you should go and help you to find rest in me. Do not lean on your own understanding. Seek me and you will find a straight path unburdened by the cares of the world.

Proverbs 3:5; Matthew 6:25-34; Matthew 11:28-30

SORROW

I see your tears and weep with you. Your sorrow does not go unnoticed as I sit at the right hand of the Father. I am not a distant God but deeply compassionate, and I see the suffering you are enduring. At the rising of the sun each day, I bring my hope. As sure as the sun sets at the end of the day, I bring my hope. As I walk through each day with you, I bring you my hope. Sorrow has befriended you desiring to overtake you. Sorrow stands at the gate of your heart to consume your thoughts and alter your perspective. The hope that I daily bring you is my gift to you that you can unwrap as you read my Word and focus on my promises. Mourning is meant for a day because my joy comes new every morning. Cast your sorrow upon me in exchange for my peace. This is not a test to endure but a life to be lived dependent upon me.

Psalm 18:6; Psalm 30:5; 2 Corinthians 1:3-4

Sorrow

I have caught your tears and sown them into my heart. I have not abandoned or forsaken you in your sorrow. I know your pain and weep over your heartbreak. I had a close friend, Lazarus who died. My friends told me that he was very ill but my Father told me to wait to go to him. It was so difficult to know that Lazarus would die if I did not get to him in time. After 3 days I left to go to his side but I knew that it would be too late. My Father told me to wait so that His glory would be revealed. When I saw the heartbreak of my friends, Martha and Mary I wept. Their brother, my friend Lazarus was dead. But I knew there was a higher yes. I spoke life to Lazarus and he woke up. I will speak life to you and turn your sorrow into joy. What seems dead to you now will come back to life.

Psalm 34:18; Psalm 73:26; John 11:38-44

TEMPTATION

There is nowhere that you can go that I am not there, no circumstance that you face that I am not with you. Know that I am standing with you against the temptations that you face. There are no temptations that I am unable to help you overcome. When you feel backed into a corner, I am there to help you out of the darkness and into the light. You never need to feel alone and never need to fear that I will not be there. I am not a Father who condemns but a Father who cares about your welfare and desires freedom for you from the temptation that threatens to overtake you. Turn to me in your hour of need and I will be there to stand with you to defeat the allure of the flesh, the world, and the enemy. For where my Spirit is, there is liberty.

Psalm 139:7; I Corinthians 10:13; 2 Corinthians 3:17

Temptation

Come to me in your weariness as you stand against the lure of the flesh and the enemy. The enemy prowls around hoping to lead you into captivity, back to the place where you had success in overcoming temptation. I was there with Joseph in the prison cell and with Peter and Silas in their time of imprisonment. I led them all to freedom. When temptations lead to sin, you are held captive. Do not give in to temptation my child. I see the stress you are experiencing and I am powerful enough to break through the stress and stop the cycle of sin. Turn back to me and you will find liberty. I am your Father who loves and cares for you. My heart longs for you to turn away from temptation and turn to me so that I can give you rest. Place your burden upon me. I will carry it and I will carry you. As the great I Am, my power is sufficient.

Acts 3:19; 2 Corinthians 12:8-9; I Peter 5:8

Temptation

Why do you say that I do not care or am not concerned with your struggles? I know the plans that I have for you, and they are for good. The temptation that threatens to take you down will only have the power that you give it. Knowing that my power is available to you is the answer to standing against this threat. I am not like your earthly Father whose power is limited. My power to help you stand against this temptation is limitless. I am available to you 24/7, not just when it is convenient. Like a honeybee that struggles to leave the cocoon and get its wings, your trials, when successfully overcome, will help you to find new freedom in me. My grace flows through a humble vessel willing to surrender. As you surrender this temptation to me, you will find your wings.

Jeremiah 29:11; Romans 8:28; I Corinthians 6:14

Temptation

My friend Moses was determined not to lead my people out of Egypt without my Presence. He understood the temptation would be too strong to give up if I were not with him. I told Moses as I am telling you today, that I am the I AM. I am *today* who you need me to be, and My Presence will go before you today. I am always available to go before you when you cry out to me. Moses hid himself in the cleft of the rock as I passed by with my Presence filled with my glory. Today in my Presence you will find that same glory, that same power and goodness, that will carry you in your time of struggle. I am the same yesterday, today, and tomorrow. Call upon my Name—the I AM—and I will go before you.

Exodus 3:13-14; Exodus 33:13-14; Acts 4:12

Temptation

Where can you go to flee from my Presence? David penned these words as he anxiously sought relief from the pressures he faced—fear from King Saul trying to kill him and the temptations of lust and murder. He understood in his most difficult hour, that there was no place that he could go and not find me. My child, do you realize that no matter what you face I will be with you? I have not hidden my face from you, but you have tried to hide from me. I am not a Father that condemns. Rather, I am your loving Dad who brings conviction. I am the One who guides you in the way that you should go. Take heart. You are not alone.

Deuteronomy 31:6; Psalm 32:8; Psalm 139:7

THANKFULNESS

Give thanks in all things. My friend Paul wrote in my Word to be thankful in all situations. He had learned the key to contentment—that I was his hope. He put his trust in me even when he was confined in prison. The prison walls could not stop him from preaching the gospel. Beloved, there is no prison that can keep you from praising me. A thankful heart transforms discontentment into contentment. I know that your situation causes you to cry out in pain. I hear your cries and know your pain. If you will begin to praise me *in* the circumstances and thank me *in the midst* of the circumstances, you will find me in ways you never imagined. I am the God who strengthens you and makes possible the impossible. I am the God who never forsakes you and will cause you to rise above your circumstances. A thankful heart is medicine for your soul.

Acts 16:25; 1 Thessalonians 5:18; Ephesians 5:20

Thankfulness

In my house there are many mansions—rooms filled with my glory. One day you will be with me in glory and experience the awe of heaven in my Presence. In the meantime, while on earth, be thankful in all things. Rise above the circumstances that are causing you to fret. Rise above the threats, the lies, and the hurt and seek me. When you seek me, you will find me and praise will rise up from within you. I am joy; I am peace; I am the One who heals you. No person and no circumstance can separate you from my love, and that is why you can be thankful. There is nothing that can stand between us. Have a grateful heart in all things and you will see that my joy will rise again within you.

Psalm 37:7-8; John 14:1-4; I Peter 1:6-7

Thankfulness

Did you know that I inhabit the praise of my people? When you praise me, I rise up within you and fill the space of sorrow and discontentment. Praise and thanksgiving are the tools that are often left in the toolbox of life, and yet they are the tools that open heaven's gates. When you pray, "*Thy kingdom come, thy will be done,*" you are asking me to establish on earth what is going on in heaven. Praise and thanksgiving are continuous in heaven. The heavenly choir sings praises to the glory of God in an eternal song of thanksgiving. Join the angels in heaven and praise me, for when you do my Presence draws nearer. I inhabit your praises and empower your thanksgiving causing you to mount up on the wings of eagles and run and not be tired. Your praises will energize your soul and impact your actions.

Psalm 22:3; Isaiah 40:30-31; I Thessalonians 5:16-18

Thankfulness

I watch over you all day and even in the night. I created you to worship me, to bring me glory, and I watch over you as a mother watches over her children. Your walls are ever before me; the barriers in your life that threaten to separate me from you. Lay aside every encumbrance and run to me. Keep in mind that I am always with you, always watching over you, and come to me. Give thanks with a grateful heart as you remember my willingness to draw you near. Every circumstance of your life has been designed by me to draw you near. I do not cause you harm or pain. There is much suffering in the world, but I draw you near to help you through the pain. Thankfulness and praise are the anecdotes to the world's pain that seem like torrents of rain that threaten to overtake you. Remember to cast all of your anxiety, all of your burdens on me. I have already carried them to the cross. In this give thanks.

Isaiah 49:15-16; Hebrews 12:1; James 4:8

WAITING

I have set before you an open door. Waiting is the currency by which you will be able to enter. I know you have been waiting for the desire of your heart to be fulfilled, but my plan is higher. I am lining up circumstances that appear to be closed doors, but, as you trust me and continue in obedience, I will lead you through. I am growing character and trust as you wait. The word for wait *qavah* in Hebrew means to strengthen as a three stranded cord. A rope woven together is strong enough to lift heavy objects but one strand will break. As you wait, I am weaving together a rope in order to make you strong. Beware of watching with your physical eyes only. I am doing a greater work than you can see in your life. Embrace this season of waiting as I walk you through the valley of preparation. The enemy would have you think that I have forsaken you, but it is in fact the opposite. I have come alongside you weaving the rope of your life together. Do not grow weary in waiting. A greater yes is ahead.

Isaiah 40:28-31; Psalm 27:13-14; Psalm 33:20-22; Psalm 130:5

WEAKNESS

My child, you are fearfully and wonderfully made in my image. As I gaze upon you, I see only my child, the one that I created, the one I knit in a mother's womb, the one whom I dearly love. Your weaknesses do not define you; I define you. I see your stress when you are driven by perfectionism and your attempts to please others. I know your shortcomings that you regard as failure. I remember my conversation with Paul. He had weaknesses too. He pleaded with me to take his weakness away, but I had a greater *yes* for him. I knew that he needed my grace and power, and it was only through his weakness and dependence on me that I could impart my power. When you embrace your weakness you will find my grace is sufficient for you too. You will *not* find a way to cope but a way to live in my power.

2 Corinthians 12: 7-10; 1 Corinthians 13:4

WEARINESS

You are worn out from the heavy load you are carrying. I see all the good that you are doing and your weariness. As a loving Father, I desire to carry your burdens. You may think that no one sees or cares about you as you go about your day doing good deeds. But I see and I can care. You may think that what you are doing is insignificant, but every good deed in my Name will bear fruit. Discouragement is looking for a place to settle in your heart. You have entertained letting him in because you are tired. Come with me and find your rest. Rest comes from within your soul as you spend time with me. There is a secret place in your heart where I long to dwell. Sometimes you invite me in and I can carry your burdens of disappointment. But when you are tired and have not spent time with me getting filled up, you answer the voice of discouragement that crowds me out. Spend time daily with me and listen to my voice alone, and you will be refreshed.

Exodus 33: 4; Psalm 23: 1-3; Isaiah 26:3-4; Jeremiah 31:25; Matthew 11:28-30; Galatians 6:9

Weariness

Why do you continue doing the things that do not bring you life? Real life can only be found in me. You run after so many things that wear you out. Only in me can you find rest. Come to me and I will show you the root of your constant pursuits. I will show you the futility in seeking after these things. Any pursuit that takes you away from me will steal your real life. Living for anything other than for a relationship with me is futile. I eagerly anticipate your coming back to me. I long to share my secrets with you, but your weariness in other pursuits has stolen your heart. Return to me and you will find rest.

Psalm 62:1-2; Psalm 116:7; Hebrews 4:9-11

ABOUT THE AUTHOR

Founder of international nonprofit Drawing Near to God based in Mt. Pleasant, S.C., Joanne Ellison teaches women to make space for God so that God's presence keeps them from being overwhelmed with life.

Driven by a vision to motivate women to pursue a deeper relationship with God, Ellison founded Drawing Near to God in 2000 and has since reached tens of thousands of women through Christian radio, her weekly Bible study, speaking, books, CDs and DVDs. She is the author of over 20 Bible study guides, the popular 365-day Bible devotional, Drawing Near To God, and Sitting at His Feet and Tell Your Heart to Beat Again, both available in 2016.

Ellison is an engaging speaker, writer and Bible teacher. Her speaking style includes both vulnerability and humor and is rooted in her passion for the Bible.

She is a mother of three, grandmother of 11 and has been married for 43 years to Dr. Blount Ellison. Making her home in the Charleston area for most of her life, Ellison is a graduate of the College of Charleston and an active member of Saint Andrew's Church, Mount Pleasant, SC.

Made in the USA
Columbia, SC
27 March 2022

58100152R00039